HELP!

and how to find it

A Success Guide
for Non-profit Service Organizations
and other worthwhile groups.

QUENT KEAVENY

1st WORLD
PUBLISHING

HELP!

and how to find it

QUENT KEAVENY

© Quent Keaveny 2006

Published by 1stWorld Publishing
1100 North 4th St. Suite 131, Fairfield, Iowa 52556
tel: 641-209-5000 • fax: 641-209-3001
web: www.1stworldpublishing.com

First Edition

LCCN: 2006906518
SoftCover ISBN: 1-5954-0851-7
HardCover ISBN: 1-5954-0850-9
eBook ISBN: 1-5954-0852-5

This material has been written and published solely for educational purposes. The author and the publisher shall have neither liability or responsibility to any person or entity with respect to any loss, damage or injury caused or alleged to be caused directly or indirectly by the information contained in this book.

The characters and events described in this text are intended to entertain and teach rather than present an exact factual history of real people or events.

QUENT KEAVENY

SUCCESS

H E L P !

and how to find it

THIS WORK IS HUMBLY DEDICATED TO MY WIFE, BEVERLY

She taught me the value of a positive attitude, encouraged me when there were obstacles in the way of finishing this work and edited and proofread the text. She shares in this work as she does in all that we undertake. Without her it would not have happened. I thank her so much.

CONTENTS

LOOKING AHEAD

I've often heard that today is the first day of the rest of our lives...and it is. So all that has gone on in the past is just that, past. There is nothing we can do to change even one moment of it. If you've never read a "how to" book, sold anyone on an idea, held an office, or helped make an organization grow, SO WHAT? It's important to know that you can.

I've heard or read many of the ideas in this book during many years of study and practice. So many, in fact that it is hard to remember who shared them with me and in what forum. Suffice to say, "I've been there, done that" as we have all heard many times. I'm not shooting from the hip. I'm sharing ideas that work.

Throughout the book, you'll be taking that all-important bus ride to success, despite the many detours and obstacles that get in the way and try to stop you from reaching your destination. Stay on the bus and it will take you where you want to go, and much faster than you believe it can.

This little book is full of **BIG IDEAS** to assist you in helping your organization get bigger and better. And, if you don't want that to happen, don't bother wasting your time reading this. BUT, if you do follow the ideas I'm sharing with you, I GUARANTEE SUCCESS.

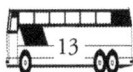

Even though I teach at a university, this is not a scholarly tome that is designed to impress you with volumes of empirical research. This is a handy-dandy book to be read, used, shared and even slapped against the desk or table when you get frustrated. And you will often get that way while you are building and making your organization productive. So when you get the urge, go ahead and slam it down (on some inanimate object—not the person you have just allowed to annoy you).

I know you are a very busy person. GREAT! It's busy people who get things done. So take a few minutes of your time and start reading this book. It can save you many hours of work and frustration. Use it to work for you and get the other members of your organization to pick up a copy and make it another tool in your toolbox of success ideas.

This is a practical book. Don't just read it. Write in it, do the associated exercises and make it work for you and your organization.

This book is a trip into the future. Get on the bus, ride it to the end of the line and never look back.

HAVE A WONDERFUL TRIP!

1. FIND THE "WHY"

When the path gets a little rocky, I've often said, half in jest, "Why me, Lord?" Then I have to look at the reasons I'm involved in a volunteer organization and say, "Why not me?" If I don't make it happen, who will?

There is a very good solution to a rocky path: get better shoes so your feet won't hurt so much.

Many people, who join organizations, do it for what they can get. But those who last, stay there for what they can give. And of course, when you give, you receive much more (even though it may not seem like it at the time).

So you have to find your "WHY." And you have to find the organization's "WHY." What is its purpose? (I'm giving you the opportunity to get out.) If you don't like the reasons for the organization's existence, you can leave, or you can change some of the reasons. In any case, if you don't like where your group is headed or what it is doing, why are you there? If, however, you see opportunity, challenge and the great purpose for your service organization, you'll either smooth out the rocky road or find another path to allow you to get where you are going. Perhaps you'll have to get off the bus, temporarily, and take a 4WD vehicle.

Study, ask questions, learn, and become an expert on the aspirations and aims of your group. If you do, the rest

will be easy. It is important to find out when and why your organization was founded. Know its history and its accomplishments.

Any worthwhile association will have easy-to-read books, charts, papers or video tapes telling you what it is about, why it is there and what it does. Ask for them and take a few minutes to find out all about it.

TAKE THIS SIMPLE TEST.

(At the university, we call it a pop quiz.)

1. Why am I in my organization?

2. Are my reasons the same as they were when I joined?

3. Does the group meet my expectations?

4. What would I like to see changed?

5. Am I willing to work toward making those changes?

Answering these questions, in writing, should help you clarify your thinking. People often say, "I know what I want, I don't have to write it down." You'll find that writing things down often makes the difference when it comes to making them happen.

Here's some information you should find out, if you don't already know it. (This will be the end of the writing, at least for this chapter.)

1. What are your organization's goals, aims and purposes?

2. Do most of your members know them?

3. Are they the kinds of things you can readily support?

4. If they are, are you doing your part to make them happen?

If you never find the "WHY," you will never find the "WHAT." That "WHAT" includes all the things you must do to make the "WHY" work.

In fact, the people who are making it work, and work well, might sometimes be called fanatics, gung-ho, over-zealous, or even crazy. I plead guilty to all charges. I am a member of a volunteer service organization. I so strongly believe in what it is doing to help people and the community, that I work more volunteer hours for it than most people do who are being paid to work on a job. I'm not suggesting that you have to put in that much time in your organization, but I know you would put in that kind of effort, if you had the time, and really believed in what your group was doing.

We all have many things we do and organizations we belong to. Moreover, many of us are very successful in one or two of them. But if we spread ourselves too thin, we

end up on the bus at the end of the rocky road with a sore rear end, but have accomplished very little along the way. Sometimes we need to develop a degree of tunnel vision. We must look at the end of the road and see if the things we are doing will get us to our destination. If they won't, we need to change the destination or find a new route, take a train or plane, or do *something* different so we can help our organization MAKE IT HAPPEN. If we aren't willing to do what it takes, and are just going along for the ride, we will be very bored and still have sore rear ends.

2. SHARE THE VISION

Every organization was started by someone with vision—someone who could see a need, find a problem, or believed the status-quo was lacking in some way. When things are going very well and look like they will continue to be good, there is no need for visionaries. People who are leaders are problem solvers. They make things happen for the better. But there is one small problem with many of them. They forget to tell the rest of the people how they would like things to go.

How many times have you had an idea of how to make some product better, did not act on it, and then found it on the store shelf a couple of years later? Your ideas are wonderful and all of us have good ones, but only a few of us act on them. Those who do are greatly rewarded.

If you want your organization to grow and be great, you MUST SHARE THOSE IDEAS WITH OTHERS.

Have you ever bought a new car? (Or one that looks good and is new to you?) You immediately drive it home and put it in the garage to protect it, right? WRONG! You drive around and show it to people because you are proud of it. (Maybe you want to make your neighbor just a little bit jealous since he or she got a new one last year and made sure you were impressed.) The same thing

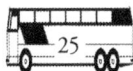

happens with other things in our life we are proud of. WHY THEN, AREN'T YOU BURSTING AT THE SEAMS TO SHARE THE GOOD NEWS OF THE WONDERFUL ORGANIZATION YOU BELONG TO? Many times, it is because you think people might make fun of you. We are oftentimes ashamed to admit we are involved. Once, again, if we feel that way, it is time to take another look at why we are members of our group. We need to look back to our roots and revive the reasons we got involved in the first place.

As leaders, and if you have read this much of this book you must be a leader, we must never miss a chance to tell someone what our organization is about and why we think it is so great. No one likes to associate with a loser and we cannot make our association exciting to those around us if we don't share our enthusiasm.

So share your dream for the future. Convince people that your group is in the business of solving problems. And that is what it's there for. If there were no problems to solve, it wouldn't exist. If you are not heavily involved in the organization, you might not see or understand the great work it is doing. That takes us back to Chapter One. Find out what it's all about, get involved and share your vision with others.

THIS MEANS PASSING G.A.S. That new car you just bought must have gas to run on (unless you just bought an electric one). For our organizations, we also need G.A.S. to operate properly. Let's examine it:

G Goals

A Attitudes

S Skills

Many of us were taught that SKILLS were the most important of these and our school system spends a lot of time teaching skills. We were then expected to develop the right attitude about what we were doing and were told we could succeed if we had the right attitude. And a few of us learned to develop some goals. If we do things in that order, we are doing them backwards and our lives, as well as the organizations which we are a part of, will:

S

A

G

If we set exciting and challenging goals for our unit, and for ourselves, it is easy to develop the right attitude. It's easy to see someone who is excited about what he or she is doing and that enthusiasm spreads. Soon, people around the excited person start to get excited themselves and suddenly the organization catches fire with zeal and productivity.

So go ahead and pass G.A.S. Teach those around you how to be effective by setting goals to make things happen.

I'm often called upon to speak at training sessions, conferences and conventions. I usually discuss ways to help build the organization. Each time I speak at functions in my organization, I tell the audience the next membership goal for our group. Invariably we reach that goal a day or two (or maybe an hour or two) before the scheduled date. Why? Because I'm asking others to produce, and I don't want to be accused of not making it happen when I speak at the next gathering. I BELIEVE IN DOING WHAT I'M SAYING. It's not a lot of fun eating crow, even with hot sauce. Because I know the goals and am determined to reach them, they happen.

When you set the goals, break them down into workable segments. If you are going to reach a membership goal, figure out how many new members you need to get each month, week, day. Then work hard to get that day's or week's numbers in place. If you only see the large, end-of-the-year goal, two things may happen that will help

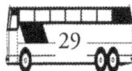

you give up; you'll think it is impossible, since it is so large, and not even try, or you'll put it off and have to try to make it all happen at the end. Knowing what you have to accomplish this week, keeps you thinking about the short term, immediate work necessary for success. And when you accomplish those intermediate goals, you'll really start to develop the right attitude. (More about attitude and skills in later chapters).

Set your goals for yourself and your organization for the coming year:

BE SPECIFIC:

I will accomplish_____
by (date)_____. Know exactly what you want to happen.

KNOW EXACTLY:

Break them down into meaningful sub-goals:

This month_____

This week_____

Today_____

"Why do I have to go through all that bother of writing them down?" you ask. BECAUSE WRITING THEM DOWN IS THE FIRST STEP TO MAKING THEM HAPPEN. Then put them where you'll see them every day—several times a day. Read them carefully and burn

them into your mind.

When that's done, LOOK OUT, because you'll get what you ask for. So be sure to write down the goals you really want.

By now some of you might think I'm full of crap. But if I am, it must mean that I'm eating well. (Maybe that's why I pass G.A.S., but I hope not.) I'm sharing the G.A.S. idea with you because I believe in the work your great organization is doing and want you to help build it. We need you!

REMEMBER, IF WHAT YOU ARE DOING NOW ISN'T WORKING, AND YOUR ORGANIZATION ISN'T GROWING THE WAY IT SHOULD BE, YOU MUST CHANGE WHAT YOU'RE DOING.

So if you haven't tried it, don't knock it.

Give it a try. Write your goals. Make them able to be reached with a stretch. Remember: ONLY YOU CAN MAKE YOUR ORGANIZATION SUCCESSFUL!

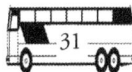

3. GETTING PEOPLE TO JOIN YOU

I'm often asked for our secret of success. How do we get people to join our organization. We have a **very sophisticated method** called: **JUST ASK.**

Everywhere you look you see people who are eligible to join your group. But how often do you take a minute to ask them? If you say you do it regularly, you are either lying or you don't need this book. If you are not asking, why not?

If our organizations are as good as we believe they are, why aren't we attempting to get every eligible person to join? There is an easy answer to that. WE ARE AFRAID. We are afraid of the little word, "NO." Somehow, we begin to believe that if someone says "no" to us, it is a reflection of something bad about ourselves. If we take baths, brush our teeth and don't look too ratty when we are talking with people, we have nothing to fear.

People say to me, "That's easy for you to say, you're a smooth talker and people like what you're saying." For years I've been checking the newspapers to find where a smooth talker is born and all I find is where little babies are born and they usually do more hollering and crying than talking. However, when I check the obituaries, I find people there who have been successful at public speaking, selling, motivating and all sorts of other good traits. So,

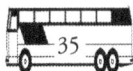

obviously, somewhere between the time they were born and the time they passed on, they learned the necessary skills to be successful at many of these things.

Some of you say you can't sell anything, even an idea. I have two uncles who tried to sell cookware, door to door when they were young men. One became very successful and made good money all his life by selling. The other also became financially stable but not in sales. He believed he couldn't sell. Yet he has been married for well over 50 years, to the same woman. Believe me, that took some selling. You may be married to the greatest person in the world (next to my mate), and obviously had to sell hard to make it happen. (I know I did.) WE ALL CAN SELL WHAT WE BELIEVE IN. And we can't sell anything we don't. If you aren't getting people to join your organization, you either don't believe in it or you're not asking enough people.

Will everyone you ask join you? Obviously not. But will some join you? Of course. If you know your organization is as great as you believe it is, who will lose by not joining? Not the organization, but the person who stayed away.

So how do you begin? Many of you have heard these things before, because they work, but perhaps you haven't done them (and therefore don't believe them). Heres the answers you have been looking for, the steps to success in getting new members.

1. Make a list of EVERYONE you know who is eligible to join. (There is a helpful mind jogger at the end

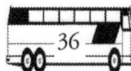

of this chapter). You might again say, "I have it in my head," but if you did, you would be putting people in faster than you can fill out the paperwork and get the check. WRITE DOWN THE NAMES, addresses and phone numbers. Then you can stop worrying about it; the list can do the worrying.

2. Talk to one new person from that list EACH DAY. Don't set aside time to go out and find people to talk to, at least initially. Just talk to them when you are out doing other things.

3. Be sure to call people on your list. You might have people on your list you don't know too well. GREAT! It is a way to make new friends. I had the top officer in an organization ask me what he was doing wrong. He said he had a list of people who were eligible to join his unit. He asked me to help him write a letter to them. I suggested that it would be much more effective if he would call them. He said. "I can't do that, they're strangers". This is a true story. I wonder if he thought they would no longer be the same strangers if he wrote to them.

Once you have contacted someone, he or she is no longer a stranger. If you are excited enough about what you are doing, people will join you. IT WORKS ALL THE TIME, if you do.

4. Reward yourself (and the other people in your group) when you and/or the group reach a new level. It doesn't have to be an expensive reward, just something you enjoy. That way you can look forward to your reward when you reach the intermediate goals and, finally, the

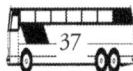

big one.

5. Make your goals known to others so they can encourage you. When you have been successful, tell people about it. People want to join successful organizations.

6. If you are an officer in the organization, set the example. Don't expect the other members of the group to perform if you aren't. Be the top member-getter in the association. Don't just talk the talk, walk the walk.

People will take their cue from you. If you aren't recruiting, the people around you won't think its important. Even people at the top levels of the organization must continually recruit. In fact, with their high visibility, it is easier for them to have the necessary contacts to make it happen. KEEP THINKING ABOUT GETTING NEW MEMBERS.

Usually, by the time someone gets this far into this subject, he or she might start to get tired of hearing about increasing membership. If you are concerned about the amount of time spent on it, just look at your group and see how many members died last year, moved away, dropped out of the group or didn't renew their membership. If you have easily replaced them and are still growing, perhaps you can put down this book. BUT—if you are having to work very hard to achieve your membership goals, keep on reading.

People tell me membership is **not** the most important thing. I agree with them, because I believe its the **<u>ONLY THING</u>** we have to concern ourselves with if we are to

continue as an organization. WE CANNOT ACCOM-
PLISH THE GOALS OF THE ORGANIZATION,
NOR DO ITS GOOD WORK WITHOUT PEOPLE.

If an organization is not growing it is dying. There is
no possibility of staying at the same level for very long.
And if you are at the same level for a few months or even
a year, it must be very boring and there probably is very
little excitement in your group. That being the case, you
will, before too long, dry up and blow away. If you are the
president, commander or other top officer you will suddenly wake up one morning and your club will be gone
(or maybe you will be, for not building it the way you
should have.)

So it is essential that you KEEP ASKING and your
group will keep growing.

Teach your members how to recruit. It doesn't come
naturally. Like riding a bike, or driving a car, or doing
math, recruiting requires practice.

I try to teach people to go out and get 15-25 "no's" a
month. If you'd attempt to do that, you would be so busy
signing up new members you couldn't get enough no's to
make your quota.

Increase the number of times you fail and you will also
increase the number of times you succeed. Its strictly a
numbers game. There are thousands of people in your area
eligible to join you. ASK THEM TO.

Finally, STOP BEING AFRAID TO SAY "HELLO"
to someone you meet on the street, in the restaurant or at

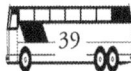

church. Unlike many dogs, most people won't bite. In fact if you SMILE and say "hello" to all the people you meet, they will smile and say "hi" to you. I do it all the time and it works. In fact, for many people, it will be the only happy contact in their day. Just look at all the sad, long faces you come in contact with. If just a handful of people would spread this little bit of happiness each day, soon the whole community would be doing it. Where I live out in the country, I've started waving at everyone driving by when I'm outside. Now they are waving to me before I get the chance to be the one initiating the contact. WHAT A SIMPLE AND WONDERFUL WAY TO MEET PEOPLE and then to find people for your organization!

Here is the mind jogger I promised: Write down EVERYONE YOU KNOW. And if you don't know the person's name just write "The cashier at store". You can find out his or her name the next time you go in and whether he or she could qualify for membership in your group. BE SURE TO INCLUDE ADDRESS AND TELEPHONE NUMBER, IF YOU KNOW IT. (For those of you who have never been in sales, this is called your prospect list).

THESE ARE THE PEOPLE I KNOW

From school

From church

My neighbors

My relatives

From other clubs

At work

From the military

My friends

At the grocery store

My doctor

My dentist

At the medical center

Politicians

On the newspaper staff

My insurance person

In the fire department

In the police department

At the drug store

At the hardware store

At the bar

The photographer

At the video store

At state offices

At city offices

At county offices

Federal government workers

My nurse

Who help me around the

house

Construction workers

Logging industry workers

My barber

The beautician

Retirees

At the restaurant

A lawyer

The sanitation engineer

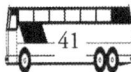

AND THERE ARE MANY MORE. I'll bet you know someone in each of the above categories and perhaps many in some of them. Most organizations have fewer than 5% of those eligible. In fact, a lot of groups have far less than that.

The 'don't ask, don't tell' policy doesn't work here. THE NEXT TIME YOU ARE AWAY FROM YOUR HOUSE, **JUST ASK.**

4. DO SOMETHING, ANYTHING, EVEN IF IT'S WRONG!

Each of us has talents that others don't have. All of us are good at something, but none of us are good at everything.

When I was young, I figured it was important to be good at everything. Consequently, I was adequate at some things and mediocre at others. I was hardly ever the best at anything. After a while, I figured that's the way it was supposed to be. Fortunately, as I got older, I found out I was very good at some things and did a lot of them. Suddenly I learned that the things I couldn't do well weren't important to me. Someone else could take care of them and I could do well those things I could do.

What a wonderful lesson. Too bad I had to live over half my life before I figured out I couldn't be all things to all people. Fortunately, I've also learned that about others. I can't expect them all to be good at the things I want them to be. I hope I can find the way to motivate them and let them do the things they are expert at.

I have heard frequently, and have often said it myself, "Go ahead and make mistakes, it shows you are doing something." The only people who don't make those mistakes are sitting back watching and not doing. That doesn't mean we should have to accept mediocre work. It just means that we should train, help, and encourage behavior that is headed in the right direction. Let people

fail. They are just finding out ways it doesn't work. Don't punish them for it. For everything you are great at, I'll bet there is someone better somewhere.

If you develop the right spirit in your group and encourage (even demand) that people take responsibility and do something, you'll get results. But if you have the attitude of "My way or the Highway" you are doomed. People will get off the bus and head back down the road faster than you can count them doing it.

I have been called an engineer since I have "Railroaded" people into taking positions and doing certain volunteer jobs. I plead guilty as charged. But it's amazing how well people do when they are given the responsibility and authority to carry out a project. DON'T GIVE SOMEONE A JOB AND THEN FOLLOW THEM AROUND LIKE A PUPPY DOG TO BE SURE IT'S DONE THE WAY YOU WANT IT. Let them use their imagination and ingenuity and you will get a good outcome.

There are people who will never volunteer for something. They want to be asked. So ask them. Ask them personally; don't just make a shotgun statement at a meeting that you need volunteers. The odds are that they'll do what needs to be done, once they find out what that is.

There are organizations who find some way to punish members who don't conform. While its nice to have some uniformity, you will never be able to get 100% unanimity. SO WHAT? It is far better to have someone doing-something to move the organization forward than to

worry about his or her breaking with tradition. That doesn't mean we shouldn't teach people the way we do things, but it shouldn't be our primary focus.

A wise man once said to me, "We are never going to get out of this world alive." How profound that is. And since that is the case, we might as well enjoy our time here on earth. There are people who feel overloaded with rules and they head out to live in the woods, desert or some other quiet place, away from people and rule makers. We don't want the people in our organization to go away because we over-burden them with how-to's. But, as with everything else, we can lead by example. If we dress and act the way we think we should, others will follow.

One area in which I teach a lot of courses at the university is that of leadership and management. And I have found out a lot about these two areas. First of all, leaders don't do things right (that's for managers and administrators). Leaders do the right things. That means they get the right job done. And that right job is to accomplish the goals of the organization. There are many managers around who work hard doing the wrong job right.

We are often judged by narrow-minded people, who are in positions where they should be leaders (but haven't figured out how to be one). These self-proclaimed experts will do whatever they can to tear apart your organization, if it doesn't fit in their own little mold. DON'T LET THEM. Remember! It's a free country and everyone is entitled to his or her own stupid opinion.

Keep doing what's necessary and allow the others in

your organization to do the same and you'll get bigger and better and your members will be happy and productive.

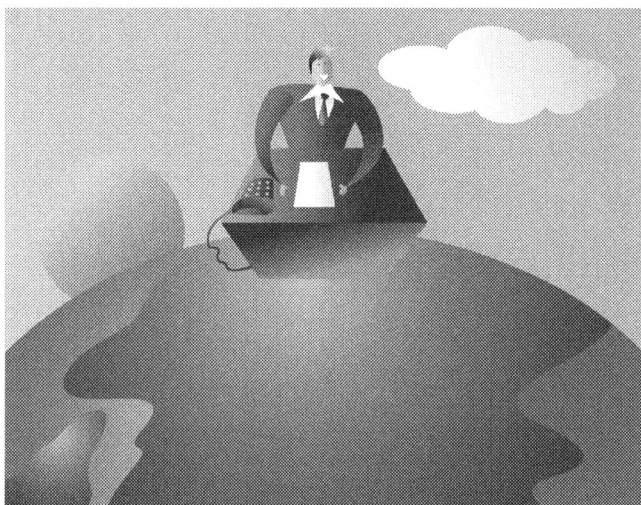

5. PRETEND YOU OWN IT, BUT DON'T TELL THE OTHERS

Some years ago (I'm not allowed to say how many) when my wife, Bev, entered the Air Force, she decided it was HER Air Force and the people in it had better not screw it up. Throughout her career she continued that thinking and upset a few people because of it. (These were the people who we used to call ROAD people, an acronym for "retired on active duty.") There are many of those in all organizations, especially volunteer ones. But that doesn't make them bad people, just unproductive ones (for the moment at least).

Despite upsetting a few non-productive individuals, she was able to win many awards for excellence. It was HER Air Force and she kept believing that until the day she retired. She still treats every job or activity the same way and still upsets a few who don't want to do what it takes to succeed. But she accomplishes many good things and sets new records.

So make the organization yours, BUT NEVER, NEVER, NEVER refer to it as "yours," it should always be called "ours." Say, "We did this. We made it happen!"

The magic word "**WE**" always works when discussing good things about your group. It makes people want to continue to be involved. Unfortunately, the glory often goes to the president, commander, chief whatever, or

major player. That usually happens because these are the people who are visible. But, of course, those same people get the blame when something goes wrong. That's where the "**I**" word comes into play. When things go wrong, say, "I did it." When things go right, say, "We did it."

Make people feel welcome and feel important. They'll work much harder to accomplish the goals of your organization. If *we* think back to the beginning of this book, *we* will remember that *we* are involved so *we* can do just that. *We* are big enough people to be able to pass on the glory, aren't *we*?

If you are still reading this book, you certainly are the type of leader who thinks first about others and doesn't worry about your own praise. *We* can accomplish anything, if *we* are not concerned about who gets the praise.

So be sure to work and think and act as though it is YOUR organization. Because, in fact, it is. It belongs to you and to the other members. If they all feel that way, your association will be the best there is and continue to grow and get even better.

This is the way a typical organizational chart is drawn:

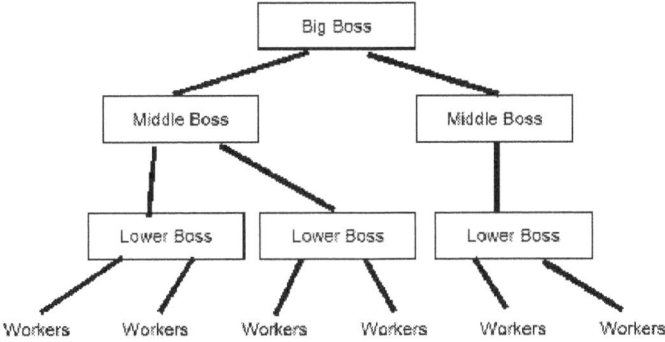

What's wrong with this picture? It seems to be the normal wiring diagram for most organizations. Isn't that the way it should be? Absolutely not; IT'S UPSIDE DOWN! The ONLY REAL PURPOSE for officers in an organization is to support and encourage the members. The officer's job is to do what the members want, not the other way around.

You probably feel you are still bouncing down that rocky road on a two-tone bus (Yellow and rust) and it seems you'll never get the things done that you should. If you do feel that way, WONDERFUL! Everything will never get done. (More about that in Chapter 10). But since you're still working at it and keeping YOUR organization going, you're on the right road.

When you feel as if you own the organization, you will readily accept responsibility for making it productive and for helping it grow. You will no longer wonder why *they* don't do something or who *they* are. You are *they*. You

have to make things work. And, of course YOU CAN DO IT. YOU CAN BE SUCCESSFUL AND MAKE YOUR ORGANIZATION THE SAME WAY.

THANK YOU FOR CARING ENOUGH TO PERSEVERE!

6. TELL THE WORLD

A few years ago I joined a local organization that had been essentially dead, with the charter turned in a couple of years previously. In the next two years we achieved recruiting goals that were recognized in the state and by the national organization. I don't tell you this to make us look good; I tell you this because we made a terrible error.

After all the statewide and national publicity and recognition, one would think we were really on a roll. We had found a smooth road for our bus and were heading down it very quickly. But we had one major problem. The local people didn't know a lot about us.

Can you imagine how embarrassed I felt as the key officer when I learned of this problem? I learned the hard way, which I guess is the best way to learn. I had invited the top administrator in the state organization to be with us on a very special occasion and he had agreed to come. Although he got there on time, it was only after much driving around. It seems the map I gave him was O.K. (surprisingly for me, as my wife and some of my friends know) but the street sign had been removed for some kind of maintenance and he had one heck of a time finding the meeting. That, in itself, wasn't too bad since he did get there on time, BUT he said he had asked several people in town where we were located and no one seemed to know. That sort of publicity we *didn't* need.

If your organization is doing good things in the community and accomplishing its many worthwhile goals, **blow your own horn.** Tell the world what you're doing. Get the local media on your side. They love to run stories showing the hometown folks doing things. All you have to do is let them know what you've got going on. EVEN WRITE THE NEWS STORY YOURSELF. So what if it isn't perfect? The reporters will clean it up and use it. It makes their job so much easier if you give them the input. And it's not that difficult.

But you don't know how to write that well or you're not very creative....etc., etc., etc. You can find all the excuses for why you can't do it. HOWEVER, I'm sure there is someone in your group that can and would very much like to do it. (This takes us right back to Chapter 4 where we talked about dealing from your strengths and doing what you do well.)

Perhaps you have a problem in your association. Perhaps you believe you really don't have much to show off. And maybe you're right. If you are, you really do need to act on the things we have talked about in this book and get your people to do the same thing.

If you don't have anything newsworthy, why would you want to be involved in your organization? Do you want to be associated with a group of do-nothings? Of course you don't, AND YOU AREN'T. Because you realize your organization is doing many great and wonderful things. BE SURE EVERYONE ELSE KNOWS IT TOO.

If you believe your organization isn't doing much that

people care about, you can be sure that, very soon, you'll have even less to talk about since you will have fewer and fewer people. All your great recruiting efforts will fail if you can't point to some successes. And when the recruiting stops, you start to disappear. Those people already in the group will gradually go away and soon you'll end up with the small handful. You will have only three or four showing up for your meetings, the same three or four you've had for a while. And they'll stay until they die, but nothing new and exciting will happen.

Take a few minutes now, and write down at least five good things your group has done in the last two or three months. I'm sure you can find these five and many more, if you really look. Who, from your group, does volunteer work in the local community? Who has an interesting hobby? Did you participate in a parade or fundraiser for charity? Are the children of some of your members doing well scholastically or in sports? There are many more exciting areas to explore and report. SO WRITE THEM DOWN, NOW! Once you've started, you'll find that it is really easy to get enough information to present to the media. Many times you can just phone in your story or some details from which the correspondent can write a story.

Keep in mind the key elements of a news story: WHO, WHAT, WHEN, WHERE, WHY and HOW. If you mention all these areas, it will be easy for the reporter to get your story to press or on the air.

Many newspapers will allow you to borrow a camera

to record your event. This will save their people from having to interrupt their other work to cover your story. However, ALWAYS TAKE ACTION SHOTS OF YOUR PEOPLE DOING SOMETHING. Stay away from what are known as grip 'n grin photos. Receiving an award for doing something is nice but a far better story and photo shows you doing the thing for which you got the award. Very few people who read the paper really care about your award, but they do like to see the local service organizations doing what they are designed to do, providing service.

As you well know, if you goof, screw something up, or make a major boo-boo in the community, you will be front-page news. Very much of that kind of news will completely destroy your organization and you won't be able to do anything for anyone. So, BE PROACTIVE WITH THE MEDIA, NOT REACTIVE. If you play it straight with them and keep them informed about what you are doing, you won't have to apologize and make up excuses when you aren't performing quite up to par.

GOOD MEDIA COVERAGE IS ONE OF THE BEST RECRUITING TOOLS YOU HAVE. BE SURE TO MAKE IT HAPPEN.

7. STAY POSITIVE

I'm sure by this time in your life you have been told over and over again how important a positive attitude is. Moreover, you will continue to hear it from successful people as long as you live. Someone said, if you can't beat them, join them. So you might as well start BEING POSITIVE NOW.

I once worked with a young man that was probably one of the most negative people I have ever met. Nothing was good enough for the lad and he was always complaining. Finally, one day, I said to him, "You've just got to be more positive." He retorted, completely seriously, "I am positive, I positively hate this place."

So much for my efforts in trying to get him to be motivated in the right direction. His response may be quite like that of some people you know, those who think the world has done them in, or those who believe it is always someone else's fault. But if you've have lived for a while, and thought about it a little, you'll realize that no one else can make us upset, unhappy or negative. We do it to ourselves by THE WAY WE REACT TO PEOPLE AND SITUATIONS AROUND US.

You may not believe that, but consider this. Two people go to the same baseball game. One is excited because his team won. The other is very upset because his favorite

team lost. It was the same event, yet each person's reaction was different. So remember, ONLY <u>YOU</u> CAN MAKE YOU NEGATIVE. It's all in what you tell yourself about what is going on.

So when do you have to be positive? ALL OF THE TIME! Is it easy? No. Is it possible? Yes, you can learn. So why would I make such a strong statement? Because this is the goal and the more of our life we spend being positive, the better will be the results of our efforts. So we must strive to get and become more and more positive and we must ask people around us to remind us if we get negative. And, in a nice way, we have to remind them to do it too. After all, we must want good results for ourselves and our organizations or we would have put this book down a long time ago.

WATCH YOUR MOUTH! What you say is what will happen. Have you ever noticed how the down-and-outer is always griping about how bad things are and have been all his or her life? When I remind him or her about the need to get and stay positive if his or her life is to be turned around, the response is usually, "Your theories will never work, look at me!" I rest my case.

For everyone out there with real problems, there is someone, somewhere with worse ones. In addition, some have changed their lives, by just changing what they think and say.

So remember, if people are putting you down or bad-mouthing your organization, they may just be jealous of what you are accomplishing. Any time you are doing well,

the little people out there will try to shoot you down. When this is happening, remember IT'S THEIR PROB-LEM, NOT YOURS. They were just not smart enough, or good enough to join you. DON'T LET THEIR NEGATIVITY DRAG YOU DOWN TO THEIR LEVEL.

To stay positive, you must get around positive people. Since they are the people who are making it happen, they'll be excited about what is going on and their excitement will spread to you.

Go to all the conventions, conferences, workshops, training sessions and similar gatherings for your organization. This is an easy way to be with people who have the same goals and who are committed to making the organization stay alive and well. I learn something every time I attend one and I'm sure I'll keep on learning because I work hard at being there.

One other way to keep positive, and probably the best one, is to listen to motivational tapes or CD's and read positive books. If you do it often enough, like driving that bus we've been talking about, you will begin to put the good principles to use in your life and in your organization. The libraries are full of this material and you can check them out for nothing. They are also available at bookstores and are worth far more than you'll have to pay for them. Once again, if you haven't tried it, don't knock it.

One advantage to listening to positive thinking tapes or CD's is you can do it while you are driving to and from

work or wherever you go. Instead of listening to some of the negative music or news you find on today's radio stations, refresh your mind with positive, worthwhile information. You'll be amazed at the positive effect it will have on your life.

I was talking to someone about having his son join our organization. He indicated that he wouldn't mention it because he didn't want to appear pushy. And, if the son wanted to join, he (the son) would let us know. Talk about being around a negative person! It took me several hours around positive people to get that one out of my system. And it looks like it isn't gone permanently because I remembered it while I was writing this.

Make up your mind today. Decide you want to be successful and accomplish the exciting goals of your organization. THEN WORK HARD AT STAYING POSITIVE—all of the time.

8. KEEP IT SIMPLE

Another well-used expression many of us have heard is, "He can't see the woods, because of the trees." Freely translated it means we spend so much time with trivia that we forget about the big, important things. I was regularly told, when I was young, that if I took care of the little things, the big things would take care of themselves.

IT DOESN'T WORK THAT WAY. While there are certain details that must be taken care of, we must not make a career of detail-itis. It's tough enough to get and keep people excited about our organization without over-loading them with things that have nothing to do with successfully completing the goals of our unit. (Isn't it interesting that the idea of accomplishing the organization's goals keeps recurring in this book.)

I have to keep remanding myself to K.I.S.S. You know that means Keep It Simple, Stupid. That's aimed at **me** not you. You are smart enough to figure it out.

There are certain rituals, ways of dressing and acting that are an integral part of each of our organizations, and we need to learn them and practice them if we are going to be part of the group. But there are many more self-imposed ones that are really a waste of time and money. Get rid of them. If they become the most important thing going on in your association, you are headed down

another wrong road and your bus will likely have a flat tire very soon.

Many people are afraid to get involved because they think they will be embarrassed by making small mistakes. When you get to be my age, 39 and some months, you begin to realize that the only person who knows or cares that you goofed is you. But, none-the-less, people fear failure so they won't get involved.

The initiation ceremony for our organization is really nothing more than an instructional and swearing-in ritual. I advertised that we were going to have initiation at the next meeting and no new members showed up. I soon found out why. At least one of them thought he might have to ride a greased pig or some other such frivolous activity so he stayed away. I don't use the word initiation any more. I call it a swearing-in ceremony and people don't seem to have a problem with it. Most of these rituals are designed to impress upon the new members the aims of the organization, and working with pigs usually only involves people who do it for a living. And we need these people to provide us with our food, but keep the pigs on the farm, not in the meeting hall.

It is important to understand that FACTS are not important, because there are always many versions of the facts. What is important are PERCEPTIONS. People will die for what they believe to be true (even if it isn't). So people's perceptions of our organization will directly affect our ability to build and grow and become tremendously successful. If we are overloaded with trivia that means very

little to our success, people's perceptions will be that our operation is trivial. And who wants to join an outfit like that?

Oftentimes the things we do had a good purpose many years ago, but perhaps the reason for them no longer exists. It is like the bureaucracy that develops in our Federal Government. The agency may have been started for a good reason but when that reason went away, did the agency go with it? Of course not. So take a look at what your organization is doing that may be holding it back or distracting it from goal accomplishment and see if you can K.I.S.S.

When I was a supervisor, I would ask new people to spend as much time as possible, during their first month on the job, finding things that were getting in the way of our success and tell me about them. I wanted to know even the things that I caused to happen. Do you have the guts to do that? You should have. If you have been around for more than a month or two, you have become so ingrained in "The way we do it here" that you no longer notice the problems. You may be part of the problem. So ask new people in your organization to let you know when they see something that might work better or could be eliminated. You may not follow all their suggestions, but if you don't get them to let you know, you may never find out the small, annoying problems that are found in any organization. Some of them may be very easy to fix and things will be better for everyone.

Take a few minutes NOW, and write down 10 things your group does that seem to get in the way. THEN GO OUT AND FIX THEM.

9. REMEMBER, THESE PEOPLE ARE ALL VOLUNTEERS!

As our bus moves down the road and we take on new passengers, we must be sure they don't get off at the next stop. We must offer new people the opportunity to be responsible for meaningful work and be in important positions. Many times I hear that we can't give someone an officer position because he "hasn't paid his dues," meaning he hasn't been in the organization long enough. This is often said by the same old-timer who says, "He don't know nothing." Obviously, by his or her use of the English language he or she must be looking in the mirror when saying that.

Many of our new members have extensive backgrounds in similar organizations, or in business or professional groups, and are good leaders. These are the kind of people we need in our associations. Many are also very creative and we must use their talents. Some have advanced academic degrees and do know a lot.

However, the smart, creative people tend to scare the hell out of a lot of folks who have been around a long time because they are afraid the new people will take over. If we are serious about what our organization is supposed to be doing, we should welcome these new, energetic volunteers.

As our bus trip continues, we may need to park once

in a while. And when we pull into the parking lot of many of our organizations we see a strange phenomenon—all the parking places by the door (other than those for the handicapped) are reserved for the group's officers. I realize they are volunteers, too, and some of them are making a significant contribution to the cause. But, if our new people are going to have to be in the back of the lot, how long will they keep coming back. How many businesses would grow and prosper if their customers had to park far away from the front door, and employees took up all the near-by spots?

Officers do a lot for the organization (at least they should) and I'm not attempting to downplay their positions. However, we must remember the wiring diagram in Chapter 5. Officers are there to help and support the members so they (the members) can accomplish the meaningful work of the organization.

I'm sure you have heard or read the well used expression. "It's nice to be important, but it's more important to be nice." So welcome your new people and make them feel at home and important.

PUT THEM TO WORK NOW.

After all, the reason they joined you was to have the opportunity to accomplish the goals of your group. (Once again the "goal" word pops up.)

Here is a little chart you might use to make sure your people are involved in something meaningful. I've filled out the first item on the chart to save you some time.

NOW, YOU FILL OUT AT LEAST 10 MORE ITEMS.

TO-DO LIST

JOB	DUE DATE	ACTION PERSON
1. *Make the to-do list.*	*Today*	*You*
2.		
3.		
4.		
5.		
6.		
7.		
8.		
9.		
10.		
11.		
12.		

I'm sure you feel frustrated at times (or even most of the time) when you see that only a handful of people are doing the work in your group. Anyone who has been in

the management game very long realizes that the 80/20 rule exists in most organizations. It means that 80% of the work is done by 20% of the people. I often talk about that to groups and the consensus is that I'm probably wrong. I often hear, "In my group it is more like the 90/10 rule." I share your frustrations. But, we have to keep remembering that we are all volunteers and that some of our group don't really want to get too heavily involved. Most of us joined for what we thought we could get, not necessarily what we can give. But, as I mentioned earlier, we stay because of what we can give.

So PLEASE give all your people, INCLUDING THE NEW ONES, responsible work on committees or in officer positions, and allow them to GIVE IT WHAT IT TAKES to make things work.

10. IF THERE'S NOT ENOUGH TIME, WHAT DO YOU DO?

Answering that question, many people, including me at times, will say PANIC. I'm sure this answer is brought about by the frustration of knowing how much more there is to do, and how much could be accomplished, but we believe we have no time.

I mentioned that I wasn't going to try to impress you with a lot of scientific research, but I want to tell you about a very exhaustive study I have made. The results of that study said that there are 24 hours in every day and 365 days a year (most years). It also proved that there were 8760 hours each year. This translates to 535,600 minutes. The math is too complicated to get into the idea of seconds.

One other discovery I gleaned from this large amount of research was that each of us has the same number of hours each day we are alive. If that is the case, then, why do some people seem to work so hard and accomplish so little? At the same time, other people are getting myriads of things done each day. WHY?

It is all a matter of priorities. And I like to think our priorities should be in this order: God, family, work, our organization. Moreover, we have time and should take time for all of them.

Once we set our goals (there goes the G word again) it

is easy to develop our priorities and then to decide the WHAT (we are going to do) to go with the WHY (we are in the group). We have to make choices and we have to discipline ourselves to choose those things that get the work done, not just relieve our anxieties.

A friend of mine called me one day and asked what he could do to catch up on all the work he had to do. So I asked him what work he was talking about. He listed a handful of items and then added number six, which was, "I've got to worry about what's going to happen when I go to the doctor tomorrow and find out about why I'm being sick all the time."

I'm sure many of us have worried about many things in our lives. But I guarantee you, ALL THE WORRY IN THE WORLD NEVER DID ANYTHING BUT KEEP US UPSET. If you are going to spend your time worrying about not getting something done, then you're right, there won't be enough time. The best way to keep from worrying is doing something meaningful toward accomplishing our goals or those of our organization.

Here is another helpful tool for getting things done (and still have some time left over for sleep):

1. List the things you need to do. (Make the list NOW).

2. Prioritize them, making number one the most important.

3. Then take action. DO THE MOST IMPORTANT THING FIRST.

4. Then move down your list IN ORDER OF IMPORTANCE.

Many people know this simple but effective method for getting the right work done, but there is a tendency to try to get all the little things done and out of the way, so you can then tackle the big, important one, uninterrupted by the trivia. If your car is dirty enough to need washing, don't do it until you get down to its order of importance. The dirt will last, so you won't have to worry about not having the opportunity to wash it. (In fact, if you do get yours done along with all the rest of your honey-do's, call me and I'm sure mine will be dirty enough, most of the time, to let you practice your skills.)

Another often-heard idea is, "Apathy and procrastination are the two biggest problems in this country. But we'll worry about that tomorrow." Both should receive capital punishment because they murder results and rape organizations. And, most of us are often guilty on both counts. Some of you have seen this symbol:

I have several wooden ones at home and when people say they'll do it when they get around to it, I usually offer

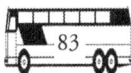

them one. Now they have their own round-tuit and can get it done.

Did you ever decide to stop procrastinating—tomorrow? That's right up there with, "I'm going to stop smoking as soon as I finish this pack." Fat chance!

GET ON WITH IT <u>NOW</u>. Do the important things NOW. And in a few days you'll wonder where you found all the time.

11. NO TIME TO LOSE, NO TIME TO QUIT

Many of our service organizations have far fewer members than they had 30 years ago. And if the trend continues, it won't be long before they will have no one. Many of the organizations have a lot of members in their late 60's and 70's and older. And many of them are doing a lot of the work. We are glad they are there and we would like them to be around forever. But we know that won't happen.

We must get new, younger members. AND WE MUST DO IT NOW. We really have no time to lose. If we think enough of our organization and what we hope to accomplish, we have to ACT IMMEDIATELY.

One of the greatest killers of good work in our generation is the electronic activity reducer and weight builder. Yes, it's the TELEVISION. If average people would devote just 10% of their TV time to doing something productive, we could completely change the world for the better. I'm not advocating getting rid of our glass teats, but perhaps we could be more careful when we choose what to watch, and when. I really don't believe that television is one of the four priorities on the list of important things found in the last chapter. Besides, much of what is on television is negative and tends to help us develop our negative mindset. Doing something productive for others will give us a positive outlook, but it's tough when we are getting bombarded with the negatives from the tube.

So much for today's sermon! But if we are going to get on with building our organization NOW it means we have go get rid of the negative influences in our lives. (This doesn't include your mother-in-law.)

A few weeks ago an individual got upset with someone else in the organization so he decided to quit. I reminded him that one person does not the entire organization make, and if he quit the person he was mad at wins. Don't let personalities push you out of the organization. Keep on keeping on. And once again, keep the goals in mind.

MAKE IT HAPPEN TODAY.

TOMORROW MAY BE TOO LATE.

In the past year I have decided to quit getting involved in my organization least a dozen times. It was just too much work and too frustrating. But, like you, I put those negative ideas aside and continued on. This is definitely not the time to quit. There are too many exciting things going on. There are so many challenges each day that life is definitely not boring.

At times you might think you are the only one with these challenges, but I can assure you that you are not. Anyone who feels these pressures is obviously very committed to the group and its aims and sees there is nowhere to go but up. And that's wonderful. Keep climbing, keep growing and keep doing the wonderful things you set out

to do. WE NEED YOU. YOU ARE IMPORTANT
TO US.

IT IS DEFINITELY NO TIME TO QUIT.

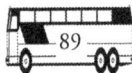

12. IT'S WORTH IT

Recently, I saw a wonderful slogan on a signboard outside one of our local schools. It said, "Shoot for the moon, if you miss you'll still be among the stars." How profound and wonderful that is. Thinking about ideas like that does make it all worthwhile.

When you see a child smile, a pensioner shake your hand enthusiastically to thank you for some kindness or receive a thank-you letter from someone in the community you'll believe it really is worth all the hard work. You will be recognized for accomplishing the goals of your organization, even though the task may seem almost impossible when you start. It's so nice to find out that those great and wonderful reasons you have for staying involved in your service organization really are important ones. And, it should be equally obvious that YOUR COMMUNITY NEEDS YOU AND YOUR ORGANIZATION. Isn't it great to be needed and appreciated?

If you've gotten this far in this book, you are DEFINITELY on the right bus. And if the bus isn't on the right road, yet, you have the map to get it headed in the right direction. So GO BACK and re-read the how-to sections of this work and keep on doing them.

IN A NUTSHELL:

The following helpful hints summarize much of what we have discussed and give you some practical steps and approaches to recruiting.

How can you sell them on joining? First step, sell you!

You can't talk someone into something very easily, but you can sure talk them out of it.

Don't overload them with information.

Ask "Are you a member?" if the answer is "No." Ask why not, and then SHUT UP and let them keep talking. Soon they will say something like, "Maybe I should be." Then agree with them.

Be prepared for "No's". Treat "no" as though it were a request for more information.

When asked, "What's in it for me?" tell them, but don't overdo it. I always mention that the main thing they will get is the opportunity to help others.

Be prepared to answer objections but don't use a prepared script.

If what you are doing isn't getting new members, CHANGE WHAT YOU ARE DOING.

You can't do something the way someone else does it. You are not him or her. YOU ARE YOU. You have unique talents and abilities. Use them to share the good news of your organization.

Don't be afraid to look beyond the limits of your building, your group, your circle of friends and GO FOR IT. I heard somewhere that successful people make things happen, while unsuccessful people make excuses. Be one of the successful ones.

I know people who have been reading the Bible all their lives and they still read it to learn more. While I don't put this work on the same plane as the Bible, for it to really help you make your organization grow, you need to read it several times and understand its principles. Then, as many people who read the Bible do, SHARE THIS BOOK WITH OTHERS. THE PRINCIPLES WORK.

If you have gotten off the bus, run after it right now and get back on.

IT'S WORTH IT!

ABOUT THE AUTHOR

Mr. Keaveny holds a B.S. in Business and Management and an M.A. in Management and Human Relations. In the past 25 years he has taught at six different universities and colleges in the United States and in Europe, most recently as an adjunct lecturer in the MBA and undergraduate business programs for City University, Bellevue, Washington.

With his wife Beverly, he has operated an international marketing business in Europe. They now reside in Rainier, Washington and own and operate a consulting business called Keaveny Resultants.

He has lectured internationally and conducted success seminars. He is an active recruiter for his non-profit organization and in one year, while he was the state membership chairman, he moved it from 50th to 5th in the nation.

He is a dynamic speaker who tells it like it is. He shows people how to succeed and continues to be called

upon to do it.

He worked for several years in public relations and has had many stories and articles published, all with the goal of making organizations successful. HE TALKS THE TALK AND WALKS THE WALK.

NOTES

NOTES

NOTES

NOTES

NOTES

NOTES

NOTES

NOTES

NOTES